Cat Count

To all the cats I've ever known – B.L.

Betsy Lewin

Cat Count

SCHOLASTIC INC.

New York Toronto London Auckland Sydney
Mexico City New Delhi Hong Kong Buenos Aires

I have **one** cat.
A fat cat,
A fun cat.
I have one cat.

My brother has two.
Two cats,
True cats,
Wild and ballyhoo cats,
Full·of·derring·do cats.

My sister has three.
Three cats,
Glee cats,
Two of them are she cats,
The other is a he cat.

My uncle has **four**.
Four cats,
Store cats,
In·and·out·of·door cats.
I know someone with more cats.

My cousin has **five**.
Five cats,
Jive cats,
Very·much·alive cats.

Count them!
All together that's . . .

HOW many cats?
Fifteen.

Gram has **six** cats.
Fiddling·with·sticks cats,
Full·of·funny·tricks cats.

My neighbor has seven.
Seven cats.
Reveling cats,

My teacher has **eight**.
Eight cats,
Great cats,

Proper and sedate cats,
Seldom ever late cats.

The preacher has **nine**.
Nine cats,
Fine cats,

Really just divine cats,
Never out·of·line cats.

The farmer has ten.
Ten cats.
TEN cats,

Chasing·duck·and·hen cats.
Count them all again—that's . . .

HOW many cats?
Fifty-five.

My fat, fun cat
Is no longer one cat.
Add the new arrivals –

that's . . .

COUNT THE CATS

1 + 2 + 3 + 4 + 5 = 15

15 + 6 + 7 + 8 + 9 + 10 = 55

55 + 5 = 60

ISBN 0-439-69838-3

Text copyright © 1981 by Betsy Lewin. Illustrations copyright © 2003 by Betsy Lewin.
All rights reserved. Published by Scholastic Inc., 557 Broadway, New York, NY 10012,
by arrangement with Henry Holt and Company, LLC. SCHOLASTIC and associated logos
are trademarks and/or registered trademarks of Scholastic Inc.

12 11 10 9 8 7 6 5 4 3 2 1   4 5 6 7 8 9/0

Printed in the U.S.A.   40

First Scholastic printing, November 2004